POEMS
TO
BABALON

Sir Mark Bruback

First Edition
2005

Poems to Babalon
Copyright © 2005, by Mark Bruback

ISBN 0-9735931-8-0

Book Design: Mamdouh Al-Daye
Cover Illustration: Luke Harrison

Ishtar Publishing
141-6200 McKay Avenue,
Suite 716,
Burnaby, BC
Canada V5H-4M9
www.ishtarpublishing.com

To the mighty Avatar of Babalon
Dina M. Innaminato
Thank you for the initiations in love

CONTENTS

Poems to Babalon

prepare for the queen
shout the angelic choir;
the scarlet concubine
of my desire.

she traveled from the depths
of hell, blasted black;
holding off the daemon horde's attack!

fighting the abusers and 42 accusers
with her every breath;
eight skulls in memorial
of her triumph over death.

she came and she conquered
the nasty beast;
redeemed she took her place
on the throne of the east.

her scars are a testament
to the pain she endured;
salvation from the cup
of Babalon poured.

Poems to Babalon

I view them as beauty marks
there's no guilt or sin;
just rose-hued embellishments
on lovely lily-white skin.

sweet warrior priestess
all-understanding maternity;
may your gorgeous hair
grow for eternity!

may you ever be worshipped
in soft waves of boundless love;
let your angel wings carry you
in the starry heavens above.

Sir Mark Bruback

your eyes are spiraling galaxies
draped in a blanket of stars;
for you are the eternal Venus
and I the fiery Mars.

more beautiful than
a mid-summer morning
more delicate than fine silken lace;
colorful and quick as the dragonfly
as it speeds over water in chase.

like rain on the edge of a storm
our passion can ignite the weather;
proud as a peacock
with multi colored plumage
shaking its tail feather.

with a voice as soft as the petals of a lotus
sweeter than strawberries,
ripe and ruby red;
your fragrance fills my lungs like roses
and as Isis, brings me back from the dead.

Poems to Babalon

goddess of the moon and of water
yet shining intensity as the blazing sun;
may we wrap around each other
as darkness
and as two dissolve into one.

Sir Mark Bruback

aum and salutations!
oh Kali
consort of the god-who-must-die
stamp down the wicked and unrighteous!
she who dances and chases away
the dead and fallen
may it ever be thus,
that thy prophets shall forever live
in the glory of thine secret temple.
oh black virgin,
your nectar is sweeter than honey
more potent than strychnine
that I happily drink;
for from thy yoni springs the universe
chalice of understanding
may I attain to the sacrament!
wonder beyond wonder
destroyer and creator
spirit liberator
bring me to death
so that I may live
from your kiss
draw out my blood
every last drop

IV

from the Muladhara,
the pleasure of creation
awakens the sleeping serpent
of transformation
to the Svadhistana, emotional,
intestine rope
connecting Manapura, cycling oxygen
and hope
up to the Anahata, the immortal
solar heart,
fill with truth and beauty
and never tear apart,
as heard through the Vishuda,
the chakra of the throat
singing through the aethyrs
to cast an angelic note;
Ajna is between the eyes
and slightly above the brow
Sivadarshana surprise!
awakens the liquid waves of tao;
Sahasrara is as Nuit
the crown of accomplishment
heavenly manifestation, the light
a testament;

Sir Mark Bruback

so as our bodies twist in Tantra tight,
the dance of Pan is pure delight
unleash the passions of the night
and may the seven chakras alight!

pleasure of uttermost delight
so divine!
awakens the snake
at the base of the spine.

the Muladhara quivers
and quakes so insane!
as the serpent slowly crawls up
and bites the brain;
the passion whirls me
into nirvana;
the third eye awaked
Shivadarshana!

your soft touches
send chills through my body;
who thought enlightenment
could feel so naughty?

Poems to Babalon

our souls have transcended
the material plane;
our minds are transfixed
in quiet refrain.

our limbs locked in yoga
chakras alighted;
love is the yoga
that unites the divided!

as we melt into one
in our tantric bliss;
we simultaneously release
and end with a kiss.

Sir Mark Bruback

V

the night air filled with thick perfume,
the ruddy clouds at the base of Tum.
as I lay on the sand and stare in the sky;
I feel my spirit jump up and fly.
floating through the aethyr,
my body remains
bound to the ground in its physical chains.
higher and higher I soar like a hawk;
overcome with emotion I can't even talk,
to describe the feeling of being afloat,
sailing the sea of stars in a boat.

with Tahuti in his splendor at the prow
and Ra-Hoor abiding at the helm;
measurement of time all askew
within this fantastical realm.

and just when I think I am all alone,
appearing like an angel,
the goddess is shown!
never before had I beheld beauty so fair;
I was as a blind fool,
made suddenly aware.
sweet smelling clouds of rose
and ambergris;
pass through my aethyric lungs, lovely,
but thou art more lovely and sweet,
manifestation of the sky goddess Nuit!

Sir Mark Bruback

VII

they kissed as two snow leopards
starving for sustenance,
high in the Himalayas
upon an ice-draped landscape,
and they ran their hands
through each other's hair
soft and damp;
it had the delicious fragrance of lilacs;
for as the great sun began his descent
into the west,
the light waves reflected upon millions
of water drops frozen together,
crystallized fantasy,
like our lovers in union
never to let go,
their claws gripping each other,
the intensity of their embrace
melting the ice about them,
vibrations of pure joy
pure ecstasy
shaking the mountain to dust
and finding themselves
surrounded by oceans of water
cried in the blissful realizations;

Poems to Babalon

and this is how the great bodies of water
were formed on terra;
so the sun sank,
sealing up the sky into night,
yet the subtle flame of their hearts
enveloped them in a torrent of pure light,
charring them
black as panthers,
darker than the face of midnight;
and this is how the universe was created;
within the dissolution and destruction
life arose from the ashes
as a seed of pure intent,
as a storm of Typhonian temper,
as a kiss from a lover's lips.

Sir Mark Bruback

VEII

the obelisk, lingam ceremony
eat the fruit of the sacred yoni
take the tincture and make antimony
as holy as the matrimony;
the mystery of the cross and rose
as seductive as the Venus pose,
the seven veils, I shall expose,
not to profane them, but to disclose
the secrets of sacred geometry
the square and the compass
and the funky 'G,'
ride my camel back from Galilee,
fast as a falcon with my Templar cavalry;

but back to the beginning,
the egg and the seed,
and there's no sinning
but the restriction deed,
for every man and woman is a star;
remember the history of the Cathar,
pick up a cutie down at the bazaar
write about it, which is the memoir,
so saith Sir Mark, the Knight Templar;

Poems to Babalon

come I'll make you purr in pleasure,
unlock the seals of thy holy treasure,
beyond what these words could measure,
life's too short not to have luscious leisure;

wrestle me in silken sheets,
become Tantric athletes,
the many possibilities are treats
that I will savor until the verse completes...

then roll over Rover,
I'm the dog with the bone,
the sypherical science,
the cube and the cone,
radiate your cranium like the cell phone;
am I doing alright?
let me hear you moan, saying
"oh baby, baby, satisfaction is the case,"
as we slip and slide into the sacred space;
the astral temple, dream we chase,
lift up yourself and let me see your face,

Sir Mark Bruback

with all the beauty it does possess,
the sweetness of your limbs I caress,
as I worship unto each recess,
more possibilities than a game of chess;

for I love it when the Yoni is soft and wet,
her light bathing me in a sweet smelling
perfume of sweat;
breathe in the sacred dew of god
the pink and perfect lotus pod,
for the adorations have been rightly done
invoke the lion of the sun

for Nuit is the boundless infinite
eye in the triangle, clit,
Horus and the all-seeing 'G,'
tickle the top of the vesica piscis;
trace with the tongue deliciously;
send her into orbit orgasm casualty

93   93   93

15

Poems to Babalon

Venus

sweet Piscean dervish of dreams
twirl through the fabric of time,
wrapped in a blanket of silver star beams
to faint murmuring of lunar chime;

dance, oh my angel, soar in delight,
float into the heavens with astral wings,
delicate radiance, shimmering bright
to the magick that existence brings;

verily thou art a goddess, surely
a spark of the infinite mother,
the greenness of Venus
at her dawning early,
the daughter redeemed as no other;

lush forest of hair, fragrant as ambergris,
your soft body arched for love,
yet as strong as the pearl of the sea,
a gift of the great one above!

Sir Mark Bruback

IX

thou art the glimmering reflection
of the sun at the midnight hour;
petite prettiness of Pandora's perfection
in soft blue waves of watery power.

for under the star studded canopy
I fall to my knees at your sight;
homage to you, image of the goddess
shining pure and bright.

I sing to you my love chants,
'o dea certe!"
frolicking like a nymph and Pan
on lavender fields we play.

intoxicated by thyne sweet ambrosia
fabulous rose tasting lips;
the soft curves of thy lily skin
my mind aflame, my heart beat skips.

I adore thee as no one other
we hold each other in tantric bliss;
worship and agape forever,
as the aeons revolve as we kiss.

X

hail! the Holy One who appears
from the heavens,
alight in me the flaming sword
of the sevens;
hail! the sacred priestess of the stars,
equilibrate the forces of Venus and Mars
Holy! Holy! Queen of night,
filling the skies with your majestic light,
hail Inanna! may I look upon your face,
may I be filled with your
ever radiant grace,
pure as the mountain snow,
softer than lace,
encompassing all in your infinite space;
hail Inanna! Thou makest me swoon;
fantastic first daughter of the moon,
Thou art the chalice of the sacred rods;
lovely lady of the Annuna gods,
crowned with great horns
of spiraling power,
bloom and unfold in my heart as a flower,
like magnificent bells that
mighty angels ring,

Sir Mark Bruback

Unto you queen Inanna, in praise
I do sing;

may I be blessed to be filled
with your form,
wash away iniquity by your
thunderous storm,
elevate me to emperorship by
the ram Tzaddi,
let your sweet kisses rain hard
upon my body;
She who makes riverbanks lusciously wet,
Queen Inanna, may your lustral waters
beget a spring
of overflowing joy and gladness,
cleanse with your salt sea
all the world's sadness;
for Thou art the queen of the gods of earth,
so too the master of the cycles of birth,
everything emanates from her
passionate pouring,
I alight as a hawk and my spirit is soaring;
hail queen Inanna! my life is a dream,
sailing this boat in your celestial stream

give me the strength all the days
of my standing,
grant me your wisdom so I may be
understanding,
and after the season of this mortal race,
let me dissolve into
your soft, sweet embrace!

Sir Mark Bruback

XII

the fabulous form of the feminine,
fills me like adrenaline,
for every goddess varies;
so I sing out in praise,
in the proper moon phase
to meet her emissaries!

I assert my right,
by the sign of light
for I too am a star;
to invoke the seven,
of the Queen of Heaven
to greet your avatar!

and when I am so blessed,
She shall bare forth her chest,
proclaiming nakedly, come unto me;
not missing the chance,
to raise up my lance
and delve in deliciously!

Poems to Babalon

passionately pouring her hymns,
lavishly licking her luscious limbs
sending her soaring in spasm;
kissing as the Kundalini rises,
these tantalizing tantric surprises
ending in the shrill scream of orgasm!!!

Sir Mark Bruback

XIII

like the soft azure Mediterranean
washing onto the white sands of Capri,
our lips played as liquid waves dancing
the passion in the ebb and flow of the sea,

causing the world to transform before me
into a most extravagant,
heart stopping scene;
then, there was nothing but you and me
and the influence of our silver
moon queen.

for we danced as children
in emerald woods
lush and exotic, passion soaked bliss;
nakedly beneath the veil of illusion
we merrily began to kiss.

Poems to Babalon

our tongues played as salamanders keen
as ocean waves upon the shore;
never these eyes had beauty seen
that which now stood before
me in my circle so inscribed
with the Holy Names to shout your praise;
not to sound contrived
but, Thou art why the sun does raise.

for Thou art the daughter of the queen
of space,
the light of a thousand galaxies alive in
this place!

Sir Mark Bruback

XIIII

o continuous one of heaven,
by the power of the number seven,
I fall to my knees and pray,
more than what these words could say,
to express my love of Thee.

azure robed daughter of midnight,
before a star flecked canopy,
I become joyous at your sight.

wrap me in your darkness,
wherein is the light;
wrestle me silken sheets,
wonder of the night!

XIV

o, dark and beautiful one
with your gorgeously strong body,
powerful and deep as the ocean,
toss me about as a love-stricken sailor;
guide me and my wooden ship upon your
passionate waves,
into your lush and exotic harbor,
luxurious vermillion port of paradise;
allow me to play in your garden
of thick shining hair,
fragrant as crushed blue lotus,
strewn about as so many kisses;
desiring to explore your
voluptuous landscape,
all the soft curves of your
desert-hued dunes,
unto the majestic peaks of nourishment
and strength,
encircling them with sweet love odes
culminating unto strawberry
summits of ecstasy;
soaking in the vision
beyond myself,

Sir Mark Bruback

moments of no-self,
the intensity dissolves me;
all about a golden brilliance
permeating every fiber of existence,
It is You!
o, great Goddess,
hurling me as a ball of red clay
into a mighty river,
sending healing dew unto the four corners
of the universe!
flowing form of crimson colors
dissolving into nothingness...

XV

by the light of the Aquarian age,
purified by the burning sage,
unite by art- yoni and phallus;
cleanse us by the salt sea chalice;
a circle drawn to create a border
we call thy angels to each quarter;
before us Rafael;
behind us Gabriel;
on the right Michael;
on the left Uriel;
all around us stars of blue,
in the column the six-rayed wheel true!
so all profane things have been banished
now may the keys of gnosis be brandished!

Sir Mark Bruback

XVI

Mother/Goddess we appeal to Thee
of skies and earth and sea,
apple of the knowledge tree,
sacred feminine in the holy three,
wisdom, strength and beauty!

mighty Mother, undefiled,
who bore the cup of the royal child,
silver-crescent, lunar-styled,
on your altar, jewels and flowers are piled;
the starry abodes on us have smiled;
appear to us now in a form both lovely
and mild!

inflame the mind with prayer
in grateful anticipation;
invoke the fantastic feminine flare
into physical creation!

bring Her in sexy robes of silk
or an ultra hot bikini;
supple breasts for milk
delicious, dazzling Dakini.

Poems to Babalon

intelligent with compassion
and spicy like paprika,
skilled in the arts of making love,
I call you forth, tantrika!

voluptuous body of passion,
with sensually strong thighs,
lotus-soft skin of seduction
arched in orgasmic cries!

shower you with roses,
masterfully massage you for hours,
twisting in our tantric poses
on a bed of perfumed flowers.

kissing all your sensitive spots
softly nibbling your nipple-ness;
playfully licking in areola-action
as your firm ass I caress.

your throbbing yoni beckons me
for my firm phallus to slide-in;
pouring lush full amrita dew
sacred lovers to confide in.

Sir Mark Bruback

soaring like angels in our bliss
with passionate perspiration;
no longer two but one, we kiss
in ecstatic infatuation.

over-flowing like a waterfall,
floating in this joyful pleasure;
waves of ecstasy overwhelm us
as we unlock the sacred treasure.

orgasm after orgasm
pulsing in pure delight;
dissolving into no-thing-ness
as rainbow rays of light!

XVIII

13 times a year
she bleeds but does not die;
a powerful flowing
as the Nile,
as the great Ganges,
as the mighty Mississippi,
subtly shaping the shores,
her sacrifice has been accepted,
deemed worthy by the Great One,
creator of us all;
for from her yoni
more blood has been given up
than all the lambs and sheep
slaughtered on the altars of old Israel,
and that was much;
harmonized with the universe,
cycling sister
in tune with the moon,
she bleeds
but does not die!

Sir Mark Bruback

XVIII

like an angel, she's descending,
ivory-hued, feathers bending;
rainbow rays of joy ascending
eternal, one and never-ending!

floating in gorgeous garments, silk
emerald-toned and trimmed in gold;
bearer of the mother's milk
just, as the saints of old.

one's experience is proof
as one's angel soars through the sky;
armed with the sword of truth
carrying the banner of freedom high.

love and will are all that matters
what once was lost has now been found;
be a fortress, the profane scatters!
as the angelic choir strongly sounds.

the visor equipped, diamond clarity
to view the future and the past;
why the world teacher rarity?
bring one, who speaks love, fast!

XIX

behind my angel seven more,
loud as lightning's thunder cracks!
girt with the steel to set the score,
titanium armor deflects attacks.

each archangel leads battalion support,
93 angels knightly geared;
riding cloud horses from heaven's court,
'just' what the profane feared.

all 93 hold a golden shield,
courageously wielding a warrior's lance;
majestically displayed on the azure field
God's glory gleams at every glance!

651 pairs of wings fly
all around us and above;
raining blessings from the sky
to bring us peace and love.

16 more wings join the fray
my angel and the seven;
in turn, we all kneel and pray
with the messengers from heaven.

Sir Mark Bruback

XX

meditation gets me calm and still
yet, like a painting from Dali,
psychedelic and surreal
as I worship kali.

existence the canvas I passionately paint
fluid as Syrilic,
devoted as Ramakrishna the saint,
spreading on my acrylic.

Dharana on a copper yantra,
the feminine within;
liberation through Tantra
destroys all guilt and sin.

my spine a phallus, brain a yoni
the vital force to bring;
Pranayama is stoney -
the coiled snake about to spring!

straight through the Shashumna it flows
this electric current;
the thousand petaled lotus grows
fear no longer a deterrent.

XXI

dive in like a swimming pool,
into the calm refreshing spring;
energize with the liquid fuel
that only love can bring.

as a dolphin, swim thee on,
coursing through the currents;
mystery of Babalon,
alchemical occurrence.

loose yourself within the leagues
of the sacred H_2O;
rise up out of the torrent abyss
to become the captain Nemo.

to will, to dare, to know
(sign of silence)
as above, so below,
find your center,
Taoist flow.

Sir Mark Bruback

like the tide to the shore,
water - waves of wonder;
past, present, forever more,
fortified ship of karma.

the wheel of Dharma crescendos,
as I pray like a mantis
unto the generations
who all came from Atlantis.

as we sail the boat of a million years,
manifold messages in water,
casting out all doubts and fears,
ebb and flow, mother and daughter.

influenced by the lunar queen
on this silky smooth ride,
above the Maya of what's seen,
this fluctuating tide.

never stale like a pond,
fluid as a river,
love: the ultimate bond,
compassionate giver.

Poems to Babalon

mighty mammal under the sea,
freedom floats the sail;
focused frenzy, flying free,
wandering wonder whale.

the hidden spring of all that's known
and unknown, aloof? alone? I'm gone;
ecstatic whirlpool of unity shown -
lustful lady Babalon!

Sir Mark Bruback

XXII

confident and courageous,
she climbs onto the lion;
nakedly leaning in luxury,
merrily marauding
on the Mount of Zion.

her powerful woman thighs
strongly saddle the golden fur;
quivering, her firm round ass
brings both of them to purr.

with a moan she grabs the mane
and bites her lip in bliss;
the passion drives the beast insane,
as she sensually starts to kiss

his lion ears and neck and face
her grinding opens a saturating sea
from between her legs; the lion begs
And roars in ecstasy.

Poems to Babalon

like the son, so rises the lion's pride,
swelling with kingly might,
then seductively sliding in
uttermost delight.

her beautiful breasts are bouncing,
as they create the sacred fire,
poetically and playfully pouncing
in the throes of delicious desire.

in and out of consciousness
in pleasing pleasure creation;
over the top, they both explode
in orgasmic revelation!

Sir Mark Bruback

XXIII

the Hegemon conducts the candidate
through the mysteries,
over the mightiest mountains
And through the deepest seas.

between the twin pillars
that stretch like oaks into the sky,
balanced in Ma'at's scales
towards where the angels fly

a symbiotic circle of harmony,
one chain of many links,
thou hast answered correctly
the riddle of the Sphinx.

born of God who did create
all the living powers,
as you circumambulate
past all the guardians of the towers,

eventually brought to the east
where is the Master's station,
to partake of the ritual feast
of your first initiation.

Poems to Babalon

XXIV

Bumble Bee darts to and fro
to find that sacred flower;
drawn by an unseen force
guided by that Divine power;

ambrosial pollen rises up
an offering to its mate;
like a web the Bumble Bee
is wrapped into its fate;

sweet scent of floral amrita
and vibrant, vivacious, violet hue
stirs the heart of our winged friend
as they dive in the delicious dew;

firm, the stinger finds the spot
and slowly slides in tender fashion;
caught in the cotton candy caress
of the perfumed petals passion

in the sacred rhythm of nature,
the Bumble Bee draws within its being;
the sacred soma sensation
of the flower's effervescent freeing;

Sir Mark Bruback

the Bumble Bee intoxicated
in orgasmic infatuation;
bounds with beauty's binding bond
perfectly poised pollination.

CODEX OF LOVE:
REFLECTIONS FROM THE HEART OF ISHTAR

"Words Sweeter
than Candy and
More Addictive
than Chocolate"

Imagine a book so magical that just by reading it you felt true love. What if it also took away your stress and gave you a deep sense of peace? Would you not want to give this gift to everyone you know? The Codex of Love is a book that brings happiness with every reading, whose words of love fall like gentle rain on parched earth. Read it out loud to yourself and be ready to be amazed by the profound sense of love that surrounds you. You will want to read it again and again. The Codex of Love is the one book that every true lover needs. It will tell you how to:

* Find that true love that you always wanted
* Keep the fires of love, desire, and passion ablaze in your life
* Experience intense sacred sex that illuminates your soul
* Be loved in all your relationships
* Enjoy a peaceful life and touch paradise

The Codex of Love is indeed a joy ride of love. It is a miracle for those who experience its tantalizing journey for it is the embodiment of the words of Ishtar, the Goddess of Love Herself, and Her White Dove. If love is your religion, then you need to read this book.

ISBN: 0973593113   Paperback   USD $18.95

www.ingramcontent.com/pod-product-compliance
Lightning Source LLC
Chambersburg PA
CBHW021227020426
42331CB00003B/507